Knives on a Table

Peter Mladinic

Better Than Starbucks
Publications

Knives on a Table

Copyright © 2021 by Peter Mladinic

All rights reserved. This book or any portion thereof may not be reproduced or used in any manner whatsoever without the express written permission of author and the publisher except for the use of brief quotations in a book review or scholarly journal.

First Printing: ISBN 978-1-7376219-0-4

Cover Image: Senecio by Paul Klee

Better Than Starbucks Publications
P.O.Box 673, Mayo, FL 32066

to John Dufresne and Cindy Chinelly

Table of Contents

Box	7
Hospital	8
Trotlines	10
GI	11
Blind Man Diving at Balmorhea	12
A Child Being Born	13
To My Shrink	14
Among Women Only	15
Death, Sleep, and the Traveler	16
The Translator	20
Big	21
Wishbone	22
Purple Vest	24
Pit Bull	25
My Shadow on a Rainy Day	26
Boston Red Sox	28
Wishing Well	30
Schaeffer and the Stones	31
Shreveport Phone Booth	32
Ham Radio	36
The Gradebook	37
Bobby Greenlease	38
His Vietnam Tour	43
Knives on a Table	44
River	46
Flames	48
Tweakers	49
Mike Tyson Inside	50
Damp Wallet	52
The Tylenol Murders	53
Gospel	54
The Broom	56
Knock on Wood	58
Chow	60

Schaeffer Is Next	62
White Wine	64
First Haircut	65
Justine	66
Horses, Booze and Alimony	67
Slow Summer Night	68
Guard Dog	70
Jeremiah	71
Karate	72
Stone Floor	73
Water Elegies	74
Leon	76
Pull Over	77
Prayer	78
Schaeffer Lights a Candle	80
What Is Lost Is Not Lost	81
Sign of the Jaguar	82
Nephritis	83
Pawn Shop	84
Hair	85
The Fugitive	86
The Graveyard Shift	87
9/11	88
Schaeffer's Notion of Beauty	90
Lucky Harmon	91
How Rich People Live	92
Changing the Names	94
Enchantress	95
Acknowledgements	96
About the Author	99

Box

I'm putting thoughts into little boxes,
boxing up thoughts, putting ribbons on the boxes
and sending them to Israel. Perfuming

the boxes so they don't smell like skunks
when they arrive, although boxes
would probably never smell like skunks.

They might smell musty. At any rate,
I'm putting thoughts into little boxes,
boxing up thoughts. I am a random test generator.

I am not a scientologist. As you know,
you can box a river thought, a thought about
the river speaking to you the morning your

father died. The box I put that thought in
looks like a little church. A church a wind
could blow down in a heartbeat, a weak church,

flimsy walls and floor. The box is square like
a church. The box for my river thought — that
I'm shipping to Israel, to Orete with her fabulous

gold earrings — looks like a church, not a
bowling alley. You can hear the river thought
knocking around and around in that box.

Hospital

Loom over this skyscraper city.
Lift a building two feet off the ground
as if it were a box of books,
as if it were a cage of singing birds.

The frozen food aisle, how arctic pole
in atmosphere it seems in summer.
The funeral home, the lingerie department.
What café waits to be opened,

what lights to be turned off
as sun envelops the city?
Shops sell diamonds, but not to anyone
you know. Sluggish this morning,

slouched by a window in a bus,
get behind the wheel. After that,
lift the hospital, your destination,
and carry it in one hand, as if

carrying the morning news
across the lawn and into the house
where two people you love are sleeping.
What next? Switch from you to I:

My stomach could feel better,
and then write the biography
of a famous magician, a woman
up the street who left her house

one morning and was never seen
again. You've been weaving potholders
when all you need is a list
of people you'd like to kiss on the lips.

A list of moonlighters, and garment
workers on strike. A list of snorkels.
But are you gathering city details:
the city hills, the city clocks?

I am sipping coffee. A sign
on the wall in the pizza parlor
said someone wants toy trains.
Who could that be? The man who

gave your father an MRI
at the hospital? Your father
sat beside you on the bus.
You rode with him to the hospital.

The hospital you lifted and carried
to the river. When you turned
it upside down, shards of suffering,
like diamonds, spilled into the river.

Trotlines

On a bulletin board a man in a spacesuit
floats in space. Ten years back, at a party
he said his wife's mother, age thirty-six,
had died in her sleep. I'm not ready to die
or to go into space. Go home—
I'll do just that when my students' essays
have been written. Moments ago I read them one
about trotlines. Maybe tomorrow
I'll read about deer hunting or a wreck
on a late-night treacherous road.

Today I swam a mile, and I'm very tired.
Also, I'm thirsty. I want to go home.
I don't want to attend a lecture or a funeral,
or shop for groceries or help a boy
build a model car. I don't even want
to peel dried glue from my fingers.
No loud music, no string music in a café
or espresso in a little cup with glazed violets.
I want to revel in my mile of water,
knowing this has been a day of small losses.

GI

The Vietnamese barber cut my hair.
Then he took a long needle with a wooden handle
and eased it into one ear and then the other.
With all the wax gone my head felt lighter.
I could have been killed by the singing of a bird.

Blind Man Diving at Balmorhea

The sky above him bright,
fifteen feet from the board
the water fresh and cold,
his body his to do and not do,
guided by his brother's arm
to the base of the stairs,
near at hand his sister-in-law,
his blind wife, and in their shadows
that form one shadow we applaud.

He rises to the chilly surface
in late afternoon when others
are coming home from work
and down the road apiece
flies circle rotting fish heads
on a lake bank, near a cluster
of dilapidated trailers, one
with a sign that says How Do.

Spring seems like summer.
We left the lake for this pool
cold and deep, bathers,
picnic tables in shade, boards
high and low, the blind man
guided by his younger brother.
He climbs, then makes the board
spring, sees by the weight
of his presence how it will be.
Then, legs slightly bent, he dives
a split second skyward, down
in darkness, his blind world
bright as the sunlit spring-fed pool.
The top of his head appears.
Fish dart underwater.

A Child Being Born

Dorothy tells Schaeffer, "If you
don't believe in God you've never
seen a child being born." He thinks
her point as good as any for
God's existence, but not good enough.
After she says that he grunts, stares
at his sunny-side eggs, and breaks
the yolks with his fork. He thinks:
years ago two men at war wrestled
each other in a tunnel, pitch dark
so they could only hear and feel each
other. One put his thumbs on
the other's trachea, choked him to
death, as the other, had he the
advantage, would have done to him.
The war made the other man and Schaeffer
enemies years after they were born bawling.
Schaeffer wonders if the
man who came out of the tunnel
believes in God.

To My Shrink

You told me I was too hard on myself.
I asked what you meant.
I drink too much,
work and play too hard
on not enough sleep.
I lie awake at night thinking of Death.
She's my girlfriend, I said.
I liked how that sounded
so I said my girlfriend Death drives
a silver Corvette.
Sometimes, she wears
a death uniform that I watch her
unbutton and step out of.
Not actually but virtually. Ours
is an online thing, I said. You
said, in person she'll be different.
How much better she'll be then
when we touch, that is, if she lets me,
I replied. I sent her
a pendant with the letter D.
I want to be with her.
I want to tuck her in at night
and kiss her eyelashes. I liked
how it sounded, my girlfriend Death.
Death and I, French kissing among the linens
at Walmart.
That might be nice, you said.

Among Women Only

No pretty girl will come and ask to sit at my table.
No gazelle will walk back and forth across the room,
no madonna with little crosses in her sharp black eyes.
This is a world without women. Nothing feminine
touches this floor which is cold and made of stone.
No finely shaped hand opens this door which is steel.
We men talk among ourselves. Here there are boxes
and bells to tell us when to stop and when to begin.

Sometimes I go off by myself. I go down the dock
and inside the freezer a woman dances before my mind.
I see her auburn hair, her large brown eyes, fair skin.
I hear her. She tells me she has a son with my name,
and walks from table to table in the little restaurant.
She asks what I am writing. I say you, Gail, are all
I am writing. Her son and husband have no place here.
I am on a forklift moving pallets of roast beef eyes.

No fragrance, no faces like wheatfields, only frost
on boxes and voices over a loudspeaker and beef smells
inside truck carts after the trucks have been emptied.
Blocks away women with big hair, backbone, and style
mingle in the lives of other women, other men. Here
on the dock hangs a grill that kills flies and bugs
to keep them away from the meat. And in the cooler
men dressed for winter and loneliness hustle and thrive.

Death, Sleep, and the Traveler

1

What's important —
the turquoise waters, white sands,
and cool shade of palms
in the Turks and Caicos,
watches behind glass
at the Madison Avenue Cartier's,
the white dog
on the RCA Victor logo,
the silence of strangers.

What's important —
Olive Thomas,
Seurat's *Sunday Afternoon
on la Grande Jatte,*
Paul Klee's red and brown
squares, Kierkegaard,
the *New York Times,*
an emergency room,
a candle flame illuminating
Nuestra Señora de Guadalupe,
the Monroe calendar
Dad tacked on knotty pine
behind the rumpus room bar
the year you were born.

2

People leave us.
Till then
we don't appreciate them.
Says who? The jay
in the magnolia,
the pompadoured televangelist.

I wish I could have taken you
to Faulkner's grave,
and on the Caracas cable car,
and last year
to the ocean
at Saint Kitts,
playground of the dead.

3

Dead friend,
I have read
Fanon, Milton, Baldwin,
and Kierkegaard. I know the score.
And what I know is murky,
like brown river water.

I have seen, downhill
from cloisters,
on a brick wall, the words
We rise in anger and love.
What's important
is being part of
love's silence,
its many rivers
and one sky.

4

My mother's uncle
Martin lived in a white building on a green hill.
You'd walk down two steps
into his living room. I saw him
in the coffin. His widow
loved him even after he died.
Then she died, then her sister,
then my mother, on and on —
He had what I wanted,
that sunken space to recline in.

The Translator

You're his sister. You know talk after burials
(baseball scores, football quarterbacks)
touches on anything but the departed.
Though some may tell
themselves they'll never see him again
except in photos, home movies, and memory.
Few think of the hospital
where, late in the night,
when they were home sleeping, he took a deep breath,
and his heart stopped forever. In memories
he walks in through a screen door, carrying . . .
what would he have carried — a fishing pole?
a football? He's nineteen,
ten years before the fatal cancer.
He greets you and walks briskly
into his room. And what did you talk about
after he was in the ground?
Not the hillside burial.
Not the tent-shaded mourners,
a few stepping up to speak of his life.
One perplexing the others by saying that
when a person dies young even God must weep.
Afterwards, in your parents' house
you're not talking about his life or death.
A black cloth covers his photo.
On a table are cold cuts,
salads, pies. You fix a plate
for your daughter. People are coming through
the front door, and the sun is shining.
He knew the word for sun in five languages.

Big

Plants were bigger than I was,
so were paper clips and ashtrays.
Still, when I looked up, the stars
appeared small. They didn't trouble me,
like other faraway things —
earthquakes, famines, *coups d'état.*
By late November the plants had died.
It's not that I was so small but that
these ordinary things — dust-buster,
pencil sharpener, TV remote —
had all grown huge.
There was the S&L scandal.
The president's son got off, scot-free,
yet James Brown went to prison.
A country where they jailed
The Godfather of Soul wasn't a country
I wanted to live in. By April
the paper clips were staying out
all night. They'd come home, big
as Primo Carnera, looking chipper,
but with circles underneath their eyes.
By May the ashtrays had gotten
big enough to swim in.
I hadn't smoked in seven years,
but those ashtrays, round and empty,
were causing me trouble. Now
why would you want to
cause me trouble? I told them.
The salt and pepper shakers
backed me up. One shaker
had a scar on the palm of its
enormous hand and went downtown
to get its hands massaged.
That night the paper clips told me
to leave, all the while blocking
my path out the door.

Wishbone

Two-three, February third
I have no Brylcreem in my hair
Two-three
an elephant stands in my foyer
my windbreaker pocket holds a rabbit's foot
Two-three
I purchase Valentine roses
I haven't eaten chocolate Easter bunny ears in two decades
I'm the same and not the same
as forty years ago
my parents at the dining room table broke
a wishbone, it was still light outside
early summer night
Two-three
I'm happier now than forty years ago
even though I miss them
and recently had eye surgery
also surgery on my nose, mouth, and groin
and have seen a car break through the wall
of a Chinese restaurant
Two-three
it's been a while since mosquitoes buzzed
in my ear, Two-three
I wear my father's watch
and remember his voice, and also my mother's
two nights ago
my friend said
he could maybe see his late brother
here on earth and I could see my parents
since we might not get to see them
after we die

we left our campfire and walked
with flashlights, warming our chilled feet
I need to ask what he meant
by seeing them here, Two-three
an elephant stands in my foyer
a round mirror is hanging on the wall
a lantern sits in a plastic box in my garage
my parents at the dining room table
broke a wishbone
Two-three, I am the same and not the same

Purple Vest

I had a job interview with a man with a purple vest
in a city of lakes
a city where in winter
the temperature drops to twenty below
a man who could afford a down jacket
a garage
a man with a moustache
and whose surname of three syllables
is similar to mine
he wore a purple vest
and a tie that at the time
impressed me
I described it in a sentence
in a notebook I lost
while moving from one part of the country
to another, a smaller city
on whose outskirts kudzu
had engulfed tall trees
I left my down jacket
in the city
where I'd sat across from Mr. M
in his purple vest
who asked about my employment record
giving me papers with blank spaces
and a pen to fill those spaces
with details about what I'd done
and might do

Pit Bull

Lorna parts a beaded curtain, and I follow
her into the Insomnia Café. At one table
Henry lights a non-filter cigarette. One day
he told himself: I will go to India, and got
on a plane at Kennedy and flew there.

Did he land in Bombay, Calcutta, New Delhi?
India is something he did
because he could, not a story people
made to make him adventurous.
There he might have smoked opium

with a man who had a hook for a hand,
a hook that extended from his right arm.
We can ask, Did you meditate in a temple?
Have your palm read? Ride an elephant?
Sitting across from him, we ask instead

if he owns the trailer he lives in. He doesn't.
We ask about Roy Barr, Henry's late friend,
who was his oldest friend. In 1949 Roy
owned a trailer park in which a pit bull
mauled to death a seven-year-old boy.

Henry opens a silver case, offers Lorna
a cigarette and with his short, square lighter
lights it. Roy spoke very briefly
about the child's death in the trailer park
in Bastrop, Texas. It came up one day

as Roy sat on a bench lacing his shoes
in the locker room of a gym that's now
a building for social services. Henry's sure
Roy, whose daughter lives in Barcelona,
went to court, as the park's owner.

My Shadow on a Rainy Day

I like the sound
of the late wrestler Antonino Rocca's name.
Cornflakes please my ear.
I like the smell of gasoline, the touch of leather,
but I don't like the thought of animals killed for leather.

I like the sound of "bulletproof",
though I'm glad I've never worn a bulletproof vest.
I hope bulletproof glass is never my world,
that things don't get so bad we always have to sit behind
bulletproof glass or wear bulletproof vests.

Papers blowing out of pick-ups on the highway annoy me,
so do poachers killing elephants for ivory.
I've never met a poacher, though I know some hunters.
I don't understand the thrill. I'm open,
but don't think I could shoot a deer.
For survival, yes, but I doubt I'll have to.

I'm more likely to see a dead coyote on the highway.

I'm troubled by people who leave caps off pens
or fail to turn off bathroom lights.
I like being in safe places: the bulletproof cathedral,
mall, or school. Modern courthouses
are bulletproof. I like the sound, not the idea.

I like the idea of being at home,
want others to feel at home with me.
I bore people. Before a television
flanked by a plastic palm, Art said to me, "You're boring!"
Worse things have happened.

But to slit a dog's throat,
to shoot an elephant for its tusks?

Ok, at times I'm an SOB.
I couldn't get along with myself,
Emile Griffith said in *Ring of Fire*.
He killed another boxer, Benny Paret.
Accidents happen in and out of the ring.

I like the pack of unfiltered Camels,
how it looks, and how a fresh pack feels in my hand.
My finger pulled a trigger, I killed an injured dog.
When someone says Murphy was shot in a bar at 3 AM,
I ask, "What was Murphy doing in a bar at 3 AM?"

Boston Red Sox

He said, "It's not about the animal,
it's about you." I believed him,
even though he'd almost gotten in
a fight with Jerry Holmes,
who played left field for the Red Sox
part of one season,
and drove too fast around a corner
one night when we played stickball.

"Asshole! Jerk!" Dave shouted.
A slam of brakes, the car slowly backed up.
"You were speeding!" "Like hell I was!"
A minute of yelling and profanity but
Holmes stayed in his Chrysler.

The next summer, my dachshund was
mauled by a chained mongrel
he had gotten too close to.
I dug a hole in the back yard
and shoveled dirt over Jake's
remains. At dusk I trudged
down the street, bat in hand,
to kill the mongrel, when Dave appeared.
He'd been sitting on his stoop
and crossed the lawn. Shock of dark
hair parted to the side, white T shirt,
beer bottle in hand, he asked,
"Where are you going?"

He said what happened
happened to me, what happened
was about me. It was dark when I
stood the bat in a corner of the garage
and walked in the house.

I played stickball with one of his two sons.
He himself as a boy had been blinded
in one eye by a BB gun.
He never talked about it.
I heard my parents talk about it.

When he wasn't wearing a suit
and carrying a briefcase,
Dave wore a white T shirt and sipped
Bud from a bottle. Tom Massey
said, "He's got a pretty good build
for all that beer he drinks."
He watched us play stickball
but didn't coach us. Years later
his eldest daughter died from cancer.
We lived near woods and a river.
He only had to walk a little further than I
to stand on the riverbank.

He didn't take the bat from my hand
but looked straight at me,
as he'd looked at Jerry Holmes,
who glared from his Chrysler's
rolled down window.
I understood that what happened
when I wasn't here
to possibly keep it from happening,
the chained mongrel,
the mauled dachshund,
was about me.

Wishing Well

A story about a young couple
on a hill who will soon part forever
should not contain a wishing well.
A story of a woman who manages
a restaurant where mostly men
work and whose husband
never sends her flowers
should not contain a wishing well.
It should contain a paragraph
about the broken nose she suffered
when hit from behind
one morning driving to work.
It should contain an older woman
who never leaves home except for
the doctor's office and beauty shop.
There should be a mirror
on her ceiling and, in a room
down the hall, an oxygen tent
in which her son sleeps
soundly. This story
should contain a desert and stars,
a young couple snuggled in a sleeping bag.
If this story has to have a wishing well
it should be two words in a young lady's
letter to her twin: a piano teacher,
also a kleptomaniac, who reads
the letter, then crumples
and throws it into the flames of her fireplace
in Ruston, Louisiana. There
should be no crying babies
in the story, and surely
no beautiful, dark eyed women.

Schaeffer and the Stones

The stones, slate brown
with black stains that look like veils,
have been here since muskets were fired.
Some are tilted. Letters and numbers
are more visible on some than on others.
Beneath the stones lie remains of those
who died during the American Revolution,
Schaeffer was told, though he forgets
who told him. They died of typhoid
and smallpox, he supposes. He wonders
what dances people danced back then,
to what music. If he unearthed a stone
and with a spade threw gusts of dirt
over his shoulder, what would he come to?
A coffin? A skeleton in tatters?
The road is tilted. One drives down
to get in, up to get out; it lies between
the graves and the baseball field.

Shreveport Phone Booth

1

Consider the bullet hole in this astrological sign:
Gary is your name.
You're six years old.
A rubber band links your paddle and ball.
The red ball bounces off the paddle,
then snaps back. An older boy appears.
He leads you off a ways,
into spruces. In their shadows
you see a tree fort.
There are big kids around here
looking to hurt little boys.
You don't see the blade he thrusts
into your chest, again and again.
"Why did you kill me?"
"I wanted to know what it felt like to kill."
He wipes the knife on your shirt,
turns, and swaggers off.

2

Forty years later, a packed courtroom,
you look into his eyes.
What to say or not say? What to do?
Throw acid in Lester Berman's face.
Then, behind bars, when he looks in the mirror
he'll see the lives he scarred.
Instead, you don't go to the courthouse.
At home, you smoke a cigarette,
walk your dog, continue living.
Lester Berman, a name you didn't know
until you read it yesterday in the morning news.

3

Years ago: I'm watching TV,
nightly news and weather.
As deputies lead a prisoner
through an airport corridor,
someone appears from a phone booth,
puts a pistol to the prisoner's head
and pulls the trigger.
In the scuffle the shooter goes down,
the pistol wrenched away by a deputy.
What if I were the man in the phone booth?
I pick up the paddle and ball from the grass.
The spruces throw off shade.

4

I was talking to someone in the weight room.
His dog had been killed by a neighbor boy.
"I'd make him sorry," I said. "I would hurt him."
I thought of striking with speed, strength, certainty.
But with what–a gun, a blade, a bat?
You want to take a thug's head
and smash it against a concrete wall, but instead
you see trauma to the brain, blurred vision
that never goes away.
Light glints off the cuffs on the prisoner's wrists.
Flanked by deputies, he shuffles
down the airport corridor. Someone comes out
of a booth, pistol raised,
turbulent and shadow-quick on the evening news.

Ham Radio

Schaeffer writes to Gerald,

You were always interested in tangible
things: ham radio, steam engines, Gothic
architecture. I was on the periphery of
people who wanted to get the cat stoned.
Gee, that'd be fun! In my house we had
a plastic palm tree, and a dog, Lorrie,
sweet and smart, knew what to do
with cars and pedestrians. I see her
poised for the green light, the intersection
where Gray's Drug stood on one corner.
I had the Mississippi, which I walked
around, the steep rocks, a bridge
that let me walk round trip. Lorrie's (not
her owner) steward, Art, dark beard, ponytail,
raised a knife to Sue in our kitchen.
I'm kind of like him, I'm not going to raise
a knife, nor will I, like one friend a few
years ago, slit my own throat. You had
the ham radio, which I once saw. Before
I left the city I lived in a place alone,
where someone had pasted stars
on a ceiling in the bedroom. I liked that place
a lot, though people who sat around and got
the cat stoned lived down the hall.

The Gradebook

The gradebook closes at noon,
Friday, May 21st. As if the gradebook
were the big book, the life book,
something large enough to walk in
and out of. The gradebook closes.
That reminds Schaeffer of
"The bar will close at two a.m."
The bar, the church, the court,
the big store you walk around in,
up and down aisles for hardware,
linens. The gradebook gazebo
on the crest of a green hill. Gradebook,
a cave, a chapel of geologic
formations. The grades are stars
in the cave's night sky:
A for friend, C for sibling,
B for spouse. Why didn't Schaeffer
let his daughter keep the kitten
when he knew how that would please her,
Mr. Selfish? Each star in the cave
darkness equals a grade: one for regret,
others for mistakes, for kindness,
forgiveness, acceptance, and deceit.
What grade for being myself? Schaeffer asked
his wife, who'd given the kitten
to a young fellow who named it Sky,
his own workplace nickname
at the furniture warehouse
of Hoffman and Koos.
Warehouse-large or locket-small,
the gradebook is open, and he looks
into it. How am I doing? he asks
and expects a reply from the darkness.

Bobby Greenlease

1. The Gas Chamber

Full figured is what they'd call you today.
A blowsy brunette,
your small dark eyes
spoke a quiet mirth.

A Kansas girl
on Missouri's death row.
A medium rib eye and strawberry ice cream, your final meal,
you put on a black dress and step into eternity.

2. An Old Story

It came to this:
marriage at fourteen to a much older man,
drugs, prostitution,
bad checks. Carl Hall, a sport
with a five o'clock shadow and a fast-money scheme.

3. The Courtroom

The white blouse becomes you, Bonnie.
Forty-three, five two,
there's a personality in your kinky hair,
in your top heavy, spindle-legged frame.

In the packed courtroom
a deputy unlocks your cuffs.
The bailiff says, "All rise."
Your thumb rubs the kiss-shaped bruise on
your left temple.
Two days earlier, when you said,
"At least I planted flowers on his grave"
the bull punched you hard.

4. The Crime

At Saint Bonaventure School,
your gray blazer and black pillbox reflected in a mirror,
you play Bobby's aunt convincingly.
Across the desk Sister Margaret
tells her secretary, "Miss Desmond's room."
You tell the boy,
"I'm your father's sister. Your mother says I'm to bring you home."

Your compact rattles in the purse on the Packard's floorboard.
He sits beside you.
"This is my husband, Carl," you lie.
No more traffic lights, tires crunch the gravel.
A field leads to a tree line.
Carl raises the gun to the back of the boy's head.

5. Bobby

In front of our house my Springer Spaniel
and my German Shepherd
watch for me.

The lady who took me from school, my aunt,
was asking about my black parrot.
My parrot is green, but I didn't tell her.
A man in the back petted a small white dog.
I didn't look back at him.

They put me in my grave.

In heaven
trees reach over the roadway,
forming a tunnel. A sunny day checkered
with lights and shadows.

Mom is here, Dad is driving.
Our '52 Caddy executes a sharp turn.
Climbing I look down
at roofs of houses. I listen closely.
Birds twitter. I can't see them.
A hill of woods.

I spy Death through the trees.
He lives back there in a shed with tools.

His Vietnam Tour

Ask him the names of GI's he knew.
Ask him to put a face to a name.
Ask about barbed wire.
Black chevrons sewn on green,
gold chevrons pinned on collars,
Seiko watches, mosquito nets,
monsoon rains, the *Stars and Stripes*
lists of dead and missing.
Did you fire your .45, your M16?
Did you wound anyone, kill any Viet Cong?
Ask about bug repellent, red
and blue borders of white envelopes,
balconies and jeeps, the beaded curtain
his hand parted going in and out of a shadowed room.
Did you fall in love? Did you
like Da Nang, between midnight and dawn
sitting in a bunker with your feet on a ledge
listening to Marvin Gaye?
Did you think, what's going on
in Ohio and Wisconsin?
Draft card burnings, tear gas protests,
no one liking GI's?
Did you think they hated what you
were doing making war not love?
Did you watch a priest burn?
Did you pray in a temple?
Ask him his name
and the number on his dog tags.

Knives on a Table

1

Knives lie on a table. I pick up a knife
and carve in the table the words
"I love you and want to kill you."
Dark thoughts resemble knives,
rose petals,
small dead birds on dry grass.
I love you, and often I hate you.
Dark thoughts resemble rags in a shed,
two parakeets in a cage,
small dead birds on dry grass
and knives on a table.
I pick up a knife and in the dead
of night I go to your carport,
creep stealthily, and slit your tires.
I'd never do that to you
or to anyone. Anyone who slits
someone's tires is nuts,
which is one step beyond
a man such as I
daydreaming dark thoughts.

2

Like people, dark thoughts
can be loving or spiteful.
I've been stung by a dark thought,
kissed by a dark thought, fooled,
and saved. Dark thoughts are thorns.
They're jet wings
at 36,000 feet. Clumps
of dirt thrown on a casket,
the mourners' veils,
the gravediggers' boots, the shined shoes
of the corpse.
Dark thoughts
are scarves pulled out of a top hat.
If Ginger
seeks work
in Hackensack, she might
get in with the wrong crowd, somebody says.
Dark thoughts are the wrong crowd.
They're the flood, the fire
the toaster, the microwave, the TV.
Nails digging into the back of a neck.
Sympathy cards and mirrors in storage,
flowers in a garden,
shoes in a shoebox on a shelf,
pennies in a jar and old love notes.
Dark thoughts are love notes to
emptiness.
Stop signs on the highway.

Dark thoughts sing of the day
I was lost,
the right and wrong days, the quiet
days, the dark ones.

River

I'd never seen anyone so lovely
I'd never been so lonely
She was the morning

A person could walk either up or down
the path

She was the sun reflected off the bus
windows

I called it the back path because it was
behind fenced in yards

There was no front path only streets and
sidewalks

There was sunlight warm enough not to
be wearing a jacket

E getting off the bus

Long dark hair, white top, skirt

I walked to the top of the back path and
saw E getting off the bus

Morning sunlight of students walking to
school, some with books in their arms

She was the corner filling station at River
and Madison

Waiting for the light to turn green

If you walked up the back path you walked
from woods and a river behind it

She was the morning star and the light
shone in her hair as she stopped at the
curb

If you walked down the path you walked
from River and Madison gradually towards
the woods and the river

E was the center of the morning she was
everything the back path the river behind
the trees

Flames

San Antonio 1924

In a parked coupe a lit cigarette
falls in folds of Helen Hathaway's dress.
Antebellum pleats and ruffles catch fire,
a day later she dies.
Schaeffer wonders if the live ash
came from her cigarette or someone else's.
Her mother said Helen never smoked,
but in *Is Love Everything?* she
smokes while lounging on pillows in bed.

The black coupe in shade
of an oak is set back on a hill of grass.
On the set of *Southern Charm* Helen
with her dark good looks sips a julep
and flirts with her beau on a verandah.
When he leaves she takes from her bosom
a torrid note
beginning Dearest Love.

The hoop skirt she is wearing
flares at her hips.
The top is frills, ruffles. Her death dress.
One live ash . . . no more promenading,
batting her lashes at a beau.
Her body a human torch
flung from that coupe into the hill of grass,
Schaeffer wonders was she conscious
her last hours?

Tweakers

No money to pay my phone bill or buy food,
I used it to pay the fines and bail
of a man who didn't love me.
He kicked me in the face,
bruised my arms, dislocated my shoulder.
But it wasn't all bad,
sometimes it was really good.

But he cheated on me with another woman
and kicked his dog.
He broke into houses and stole things:
a laptop, a generator, pool cues, ball caps.
His dog shit on the floor, and I cleaned it up.

Texting while driving,
*Hey Deb, I found the struts for my truck. Is your daughter
and her girl still there? Fucking better not be . . .*
he hit a car head on.

One morning we got high.
At John Deere, my work, I set a table on fire.

My God, what have I done? I look in the mirror
and pray he loves me.

Mike Tyson Inside

Fee-fi-fo-fum — Cassius Clay here I come . . .
from this dark and solitary place
where no means yes, Mike, give it to me
in the garden of your heart pretty flowers
pansies white blue violet fuchsia black gold
droop like they've been beaten by heavy rain.
Clay beat Liston and Vietnam and bloomed
to float like a butterfly in the Thrilla in Manila.
I was his heir apparent, wayward man-child
in the promised land. Cus died, taking into
earth a piece of my heart.
I was brute bulk and adrenaline, an inside-
animal. Can't no one touch me except her
and her mother's looming shadow in our home.
Robin was a dream with claws. On our
designer couch I drank
my liquor neat and reached for Cus. The Prince
of Nothing helped me up before the ten
count. Shouldering chaos, behind the wheel
of my BMW I headed straight for the heart
of a Catskill oak. Even a brute sees stars
some dark night. Pulled from the wreckage I
floated through a dream arcade holding no one's
hand. In the Tokyo Dome
Buster Douglas, nobody really, proved even a
nobody could be somebody one fleeting hour.
The heir to Muhammad Ali down, not defeated.
The next logical step: a correspondence course
for my GED, then a televised chat
where I sank into the luxury of that couch,
my arm 'round dream Robin in that mansion
her mother's shadow loomed. Fee-fi-fo-
fum, here I come all you *Ebony* lovelies.
Don't say goodnight at 5 A.M. No means yes

I'm bad, that's good. "Come back to Indiana,
Stranger, but not too late." My Italian suit
swapped for jailhouse denims, there's
no hand qualified to carry my jockstrap. Fight?
I'll fight the lowliest guard, the pale fairy
warden, for free get inside pump the uppercut
puffing belligerent me. What I was made for.
Sitting in stir in the dark I crack my knuckles.
Anyone home upstairs? an inner voice whispers.
On the edge of a cot I sit and mind-rise to glass
as expensive as Don King's bathroom mirrors.
There in the garden of my hard heart pansies
petals gold white fuchsia purple midnight blue
bloom and boom — bruised by the heavy rains'
deadly left hook.

Damp Wallet

Cleaning the garage,
humid, low nineties.
I'm sweating. My wallet
in my hip pocket is damp.
Damp, the Connecticut driver's license,
the insurance card (plastic),
and the secret police card (paper),
and the Lon Chaney fan club card
(invisible). Damp, the snapshots
of two nephews: Thomas, Richard,
(the latter lost a finger in a university
shop class). Damp, the part of me
that extends to the varied bureaus.
Tonight, before bed, I'll place it
on top my chest of drawers.
I'd like to tell people it got soaked
when I dove into the river
to save the blind child who'd
been playing on its curved,
grassy bank and had slipped
and been taken by the current.
Or that it got soaked at a pool
party by splashers who thought
their splashes gestures of affection,
and that it was my pool.
I'd like to tell people the man
who lives in my wallet is not me,
but another, a university wood
shop instructor who knows
what to do and who to call
if someone loses a finger, or more.

The Tylenol Murders

May 13, 1994

Managing editor
Chicago Tribune
160 N. Stetson Ave.
Chicago, IL 60601

Dear editor,

Who's to catch me? That won't happen.
I live it over and over,
putting cyanide in capsules, capsules
in a container, the container in a box,
so the box sits on a shelf like it's never
been opened. Then a girl opens it;
a twelve-year-old girl at home
fills a water glass, swallows Tylenol
and within three hours dies.

You wonder someone lusts
to take a human life, but not hear a gasp
or see a twinge, or a shudder,
at the bedside, the father, or a nurse.
Never caught. Who could I be?
A man having dinner with his mother
in their Evanston apartment?
A woman from Glencoe,
listening to Spyro Gyra at Ravinia?

Print or trash my letter.
You have no one to hate, no one
to scream at in court as the survivor
of the serial rapist might scream,
or the father of the twelve-year-old
who was buried might scream: monster!
I did this. Someone will find out
I put the boxes
back on shelves in Winnetka, in 1982.

Gospel

Schaeffer writes to Tasia:

"Rhythm & blues, nothing like it!
The languid lovely haunting sound
I heard back then, and now
when I see music I see a long
narrow shop, walls lined with
45 vinyl discs sometimes red
or yellow, mostly black, inlaid
with labels: blue, green, pink,
black, and names: Chance, Duke,
Peacock, Checker, a montage
of color and design. Up front
across a counter sat Dennis:
dark eyes, rosy cheeks, sensuous lips
and a few thin cowlicks spilled
partly down his forehead. Dennis
knew R&B very well, not
R&B as we hear today, but stuff
from the late 40's, early 50's.
He was fortunate to be at the heart
of all those languid melodies,
not jump tunes, but the ballads."

Schaeffer saw him in later years
only once before Dennis passed.
A different record shop, where both
were visitors. Dennis's opened black
leather revealed a waist that had
thickened, and instead of rosy cheeks
there was a puffiness to his face.
Somehow gospel came up in their
talk, Schaeffer said the Swan Silvertones
to which Dennis replied, Oh,
they're the best, a wry smile

in his eyes. Schaeffer felt he'd
been right all along, these past
few years, since he began listening
to gospel, that the Swan Silvertones
with their tenor lead Claude Jeter
were the best. Dennis corroborated
Schaeffer's feeling. He thinks —
when he sees Dennis up front in
a corner of the long narrow shop —
music is feeling, you feel the music.

The Broom

During the Cold War
between laundry, dusting, and vacuuming
my mother stopped to smoke a Chesterfield.
She took one from the pack, with its gold doodad
like a square lamppost on a street of off-white city snow.
They're not made anymore, so to carry on the name
I'll name myself Paul Chesterfield.
I'll write essays readers will act on, for example,
one about a river you wouldn't want to jump in
much less get thrown in. If someone says
to his friends, Let's throw Paul in the river,
I'll beg them not to. Rats, and gars with razor teeth
lurk under the surface. I wouldn't want to be bitten,
slashed, or stung as I struggled to the sludgy shore.
I'll write about the river and spur my readers to act
so in no time the water will be clear enough
to stand in shallows and see your feet,
because of my essay. Too bad my mother isn't here
to witness what might be her son's triumph.
She wasn't a heavy smoker, a pack would last a week
and, in later years she switched to Salem lights
like smoking air for Pete's sake, a pack might last
a month, though she herself didn't last too long.
As Paul Chesterfield I wouldn't write about death.
No death and dying, but I'd write about violence
in schools, not the metal detectors of today
or teachers armed with concealed .38s, but Cold War
school violence. Scared to . . . no, not the D word,
scared out of my wits, I'd cringe. Teachers exploded
into flailing arms, grasping hands, their eyes, their voices!
None were like Mr. Rogers or Ward Cleaver.
Faces slapped, forearms bruised, hair pulled, shins kicked.
Cold War teachers, some of you, I'm sure, are still
among us. As Paul C. I'd write about school violence,
and Cold War gardening, and the morning

I threw a broom at Frank Baronowski, my foreman
at Star Meats. I was in my mid-twenties,
and the VP, Lloyd Siegel, who's taking it all in,
pulls me aside. Paul, so out of character!
How I wanted to explain what led up to it!
But I stood there, with Lloyd's eyes working me over,
as if he were Marciano and I, Paul C.
author of "The Broom," just a sparring partner,
a few rounds of work before the real fight.

Knock on Wood

The silver transistor at Dunn's feet blared
Eddie Floyd.
"If I do I would surely lose a lot."
Dunn, a bear of a man, teased
staccato rhythms from the radio.
"I'm not superstitious . . ."

Camp Tien Sha was low white buildings,
a swath of trees, at the end
of an unpaved road, Monkey Mountain
greener than Dunn's fatigues as he
danced on the walk outside the barracks
that Sunday night in August.

"Think I better knock, knock . . ."
Dunn's big dark body tiptoed, slid,
shuffled, swayed to the music. In Vietnam
I paced in the dark, and sat
in a shack walled by sandbags
with an M16 near at hand. I turned twenty.

People passed by: Dunn, the heavy dancer;
Tan, the guard we "caught" squatting,
his feet on the commode lid, his way
different from ours, we Americans;
Moore, the young Californian Rorie
and other New Yorkers wanted to smack,
because of where he was from.

I liked the motion of riding in an open Jeep,
hard yet soft, casual.
I saw the dull green of the Jeeps,
their sides filmed with dust;
wood slats of a barracks,
its balcony's long wooden rail;
lines of men with silver trays
in the mess hall; faces:
Mai the laundry girl's round pale face,
her short permed hair; the long brown face
of Ackles, a GI from Pittsburgh.

An early Sunday night, mountains
behind us, Dunn, big and very dark,
danced on the walk
in front of our barracks, danced
in his light green fatigues.
His body moved gracefully.
He can dance, I thought.
I watched him all of thirty seconds.

Chow

A summer night crowded sidewalk,
the big lighted windows of the ice cream
parlor on the corner.
A dark-haired girl
in a long skirt walks a rust-colored chow.
"As a child," he said, "I was frightened
by a chow." There was a train,
the upper west coast in his story.
I remember his comb-over,
turtleneck, black bicycle, dark frame
glasses, the gaunt cheeks,
blue eyes flushed with cataract.
"I was frightened." I didn't ask,
Scared shitless? He didn't slang ever,
but spoke properly, and liked his meter,
Alexandrines, end rhymes,
and lived the Frost dictum:
free verse is tennis without a net.
That night, and back further,
the west coast, a train, a chow,
he was back there,
transfixed on the sidewalk,
near the ice cream parlor corner.
Didn't say if the chow's teeth had sunk
into his flesh or someone else's
before his eyes.
He washed dishes, though I never saw
him at work, a white apron,
damp towel drying a dish for a paycheck.
Only saw the wine-red turtleneck,
always the long stem pipe
in the corner of his mouth, except he
took it out to recite Valery
or something from Homer. He liked
Wilbur, Hecht, abhorred free verse.
Ginsberg and Bly weren't for him,
nor was the dishtowel, the apron.

I see him walking his bike on a sidewalk.
I see him, too, on that summer night
of the chow. I remember his voice,
the bowl in his hand of the long stem pipe
suspended in air as he spoke lines from
"To Helen." "O azure one . . ."
I'm frightened of going to sleep
and never waking, or withering in some
neverland, by a window,
not even cognizant of wall or window.
Someone asks, "Do you know what you're
sitting in?" "Say chair."
I'm frightened of the car wreck,
the anything that'll take me. Take my
last breath, and that's it.
Like the morning S.C. woke thinking
it'd be an average day
and keeled over near the back
of a pickup she was helping a friend with.
What after the turtleneck,
the cloudy eyes behind the dark rim
glasses, the comb-over,
pipe in the corner of the mouth long
and thin,
the man whose voice is clear in memory,
to whom I cannot say,
you are extinct, you are nothing, less
than a strip of grout between tiles
in a bathroom toilet. You are no more,
to whom poetry meant everything,
all formalism, the real thing
in lines you left in journals a few
people open and read.
No more chow to be frightened of.
That summer night crowded sidewalk,
the backs of people at stools
in the well-lit ice cream parlor, one
spoons a dollop of ice cream,
raises it to his mouth.

Schaeffer Is Next

The next vape, the next corner
to turn, the next day, he drove
to Maidenrock. It was a Saturday.
Schaeffer thinks of the adjective,
then, next, please, please added
to soften the blow that one is next,
whether one likes it or not. Schaeffer
thinks, I'm next. He thinks:
the next vampire film, the next
trip to Walmart, the next bite
of the apple, the next diver
to leap from the plane and pull
the parachute string to soften the fall.

Don't sit under the apple tree
with anyone else but Kim Kardashian West.
Don't sit under the apple tree
with anyone but Derek Jeter
with anyone but Taylor Swift
with anyone but a descendant of Clyde
Barrow, with anyone whose surname
is Lake.
Don't do it, don't sit there with
Casey Anthony, Susan Smith
or Charles Manson.

The next vape, the next hero,
the next vampire, the next banquet,
the next moment, who knows,
anything might happen:
a river might flood,
a tree might catch on fire.

There's the Rita H angle,
how she was glamorous in her voice,
her eyes, her long wavy red hair,
her spangled dress that hugged her hips.
Glamorous in her walk, in how she moved
back and forth on stage
under the spotlight in *Gilda*.
Then, spin the wheel of time forward,
say, twenty years and find her
alone in a room. Dementia
has taken over.
She is cared for, incontinent,
can't wipe herself or wash her
once lovely hair. Oh,
the waking nightmare bird
perches on her shoulder
that was once bare and aflame
with lust, all of her.

White Wine

I pictured myself a gray-haired forty,
vacuuming a rug,
a glass of white wine
in one hand, in my mouth a menthol 100.
I pictured myself old
and small with a glass of white wine,
climbing Everest; patient and young
with a glass of white wine, dining on shark
charbroiled on Bastille Day;
middle aged and impulsive with a glass of white wine,
spelunking in Carlsbad; young and curious
with white wine, hunting ducks in November;
old and compassionate, convalescing
from knee surgery on a porch with white wine,
looking out at sage and mesquite, looking up
at the big sky empty of buzzards at 10 am;
with my glass of white wine, in the stands,
middle aged and excited, supporting the Celtics
as the buzzer sounds.

First Haircut

In the small shop, in his mother's lap,
scissors clipping his fine
three years old hair,
he won't remember mirrors,
the electric razor, the barber's hand,

but something of this hour,
like a memory of first steps
or some other early childhood first,
may come back.
Such moments light the dark hour
we fade from loved ones and all things.
For him, may that time be far off.

His mother's pride,
he keeps cool under the strange blade.

Justine

We're singing "Don't Play the Game."
Our choir director Tanner Wilkins looks
straight at me at our rehearsal
for Sunday service when somebody
who looks like my sister Judy will stand
in the baptismal font above the pulpit
so people in pews can see the person,
dunked by Pastor McCall, come up wet,
and, at the service's end, stand while
the faithful form a line and one by one
shake the baptized person's hand.
When that happened to me, earlier
that day I had fallen and scraped my hand,
playing tennis with Kayla, my and Judy's
roommate. The faithful shook my hand
and it hurt, but I had this glow, a halo
about me in my mind and in theirs.
Pain, that night, was nothing. I was saved.
Tonight Tanner looks daggers at me.
We're singing "Don't Play the Game."
Look at Kayla, I'm thinking, who not only
is not in the choir but is also not saved, though
she looks saved, like a PTA treasurer.
Behind her closed door she likes it
when Andy, her boyfriend, calls her names.
Her face flushes, her breaths quicken,
she told me. She doesn't tell all, but
who does? Tanner has two daughters.
Jimmie, the elder, I heard talk about
one night in George's Beer Garden.
Three guys one table over from mine.
Jimmie this, Jimmie that. I'm sure
it was Tanner's daughter. So, look at her,
look her in the eye. Don't play the game!

Horses, Booze, and Alimony
(Got All Your Money)

Homer Dunn 1935–1978 sang with the R & B group The Rivieras, whose 45 record "Moonlight Serenade" rose to number 47 on the Hit Parade in 1959.

You smoked occasionally, laughed often.
And I'm tempted here, miles from your grave,
to refuse to do the next chore,
take the next breath or turn the next corner.
Bones crumbling, you're all voice now.
Is there room for your voice,
room enough in the coffin,
room enough in the house?

I should sing you a song
but I can't sing or dance.
I can't keep the peace with people too well
the way you could. Nevertheless, the world turned
and bit you. I see you
standing before glass doors,
that row of stores where you worked
mopping floors of a supermarket,
where I loitered my teen years,
and where we met.

Your hands touch metal carriages
the way a pianist's hands touch keys.
I should build a palace for your voice.
I should buy an opal pin
for your black four-in-hand, get out of this
completely, and let you take over.

Slow Summer Night

Alisha, behind the counter,
at Come'n'Go,
smiles as he pays for gas and tells her
her face is interesting. "I'm Bob."
What else can he tell her?

She wonders if they'd like each other.
Interesting, not boring.
Boredom is good.
It's the beginning of restlessness and
restlessness leads to house painting,
hiking, moving furniture and,
as they say in Australia, the spinning of
yarns.
She gives him his American Express,
and says, "Alisha,"
extending her hand to his hand,
saying nothing about Doubt,
which is what this town is called,
saying nothing about
her warped porch,
her lawn of Johnson grass and weeds,
the two churches,
the high rate of teen pregnancy,
the river alongside the football field.
Once, out of love, she rode a Greyhound
two thousand miles to her sister's
wedding.
Bob, he said. "I'm Bob."

Alisha reads — *Man Sucked Out of Somali
Airliner After Inflight Explosion.*
He killed himself only, the *Record* reports,
while injuring two others. Somali
detectives question
airport baggage handlers.

She unclasps a barrette.
Her hair falls to her shoulders. Outside,
Bob's Taurus pulls away,
leaving a swirl of exhaust in the dark.

Guard Dog

I knew a chained dog, his chain thick
and rusty. Timidly I petted him,
the eyes in his face small and gray.
Some nights his loud bark woke
the people whose house he guarded.
I saw him run in their long, spacious yard,
a hill fenced by chain link.
His house sat on a platform of blond wood,
a plateau on the long hill of the yard.
His shaggy black mane sun bleached,
he was big, his mouth was big.
The chain big and long clumped
the turd-stained platform, a stage
for Prince. I never saw him with other dogs.

Jeremiah

An outlaw who robbed trains and banks
before the automobile took the road kept a journal,
and you, in Missouri, read its first passage
about the night his first son was born, the joy
in that house, even with a blizzard outside.

The outlaw died violently before his son's adolescence.
Outside the museum home where he lived
with his family and also died, you contemplate
the hand that held the pen and the Colt 45.
Jeremiah he'd written in that opening passage,

his son's name. You imagine Jeremiah
with a family of his own, in an Oklahoma City park
whisking his young daughter Jessica
into his arms. His hands, like his father's,
are small. You imagine Jeremiah's wife

age thirty-six, dying of typhoid, leaving him
with three children and his job in a bustling shoe store.
You imagine your grandfather, eight years old
in the store with his mother. Jeremiah sits
your grandfather down and, kneeling, places a shoe

on his left foot, then one on his right.
Your grandfather rises and walks back and forth
in brown shoes of the early twentieth century.
Outside it is hot and sunny, vastly different
from the blizzard the night Jeremiah was born.

Karate

He was dead most of his life,
although he didn't know it.
He did not become a father until he died.

Not old, he raised Diane and Margaret
from infancy to adolescence.
Proud they were involved in karate
he drove them to lessons.
They kicked and lunged, lean
in white smocks. It was what he wanted,
being a father. Before they were born

he wanted others . . . methadone,
coke, grass. He provided others
with such things and wanted them
to see him . . . in the car . . . with the girl
and the drugs. Eventually he married
a girl, a nurse. He wanted a roof
for shelter, steady employment,
say, behind a bar. For he was good
mixing a Tom Collins. These girls —
first one, two years later the other.

Then he began to live — as if the self
he'd been, on a corner waiting,
looking to sell acid or score a bag of smack,
as if *he* never existed.

Stone Floor

In a desert dugout the concrete
I mix with water
sloshes in a wheelbarrow.

It looks like clay with pebbles.
I lay flat stones on dirt.
Far from blacktop

and houses with running water,
I think of my friends who recently
held their stillborn son.

I slit bags of concrete with a hoe.
Rain has kept the ocotillos green,
with buds of purple and blue.

Outside the dugout,
yellow flowers on a hill.
He broke down twice on the phone,

another friend said,
yesterday, the day I came here.
Concrete dries my hands.

With a soaked rag I wash
the concrete film from stones.
I dip water from a bucket

and pour it into the wheelbarrow.
I slit another bag. Dust rises.
I pour more water.

With stones gotten earlier
from a creek-bed intact,
forty percent of the floor done,

I drive the five hours home.

Water Elegies

1

Your mother,
buying you a suit,
touches your breast pocket
and tells you to make sure
there's enough room
for your cigarettes.
A week ago last night
you walked a girl
to a duck pond
not far from this shop.
You walked her home.
Two days later
you saw her with another boy.
You're thinking of willows,
moonlight on water
and her kisses.
Your mother lifts
a thread from your sleeve.

2

Twice a week you sell plasma.
Today, as your blood leaves you,
you hear your mother weeping.
She lost her engagement ring in the waves
and carried on about how your father
labored for a diamond. You searched
for that small fragment of your life,
then rose from the sea with empty hands.

Leon

Henry wants to take Leon camping.
Leon, who lives in a halfway house,
is a sixteen-year-old
Henry has taken charge of.
I don't want Leon to go.
It was okay that first time,
but a second might lead to a third
and a fourth. I phone Henry.

Pull Over

Pull over in daylight.
Take the exit ramp.
Pull over. I need to tell you something.
Pull into the rest area, please.

By the time you get back
into parkway traffic,
life as you've known it
will have taken flight.

Finding home, Poe's raven
perched on your roof.
Words can't silence its caws,
nor can summer thunder.

Earlier you walked through my door.
The X-rays, the lower back pain
we'd hoped was nothing.
Please, pull over.

From now on
all things compared to this
will be smaller, or greater:
the windshield, the parkway's

green and white signs
in the midday glare,
your children, grandchildren.
Are you driving? Please, pull over.

Prayer

1. Cambric Splint

The lake at dusk: a tableau of trees
across the water in silhouette,
silver sky, bathers near shore,
skiers behind boats. Our towels on sand,
Andy breast stroked across a lagoon,
and I followed. One Saturday
driving home from the lake we stopped
at a strip mall in Rogers,
and went into a yogurt shop owned by
Syd, a man in our singles group,
who was originally from Iran. Syd
wore a huge cambric splint on one hand.
A week before our visit he was unhitching
a boat from a truck. It slipped.
Its weight came down on his hand.
He treated Andy and me to yogurt parfaits,
tall glasses of coffee colored froth,
whipped cream, cherries.
At a small vinyl table, before eating
we prayed for Syd's hand.

2. Wheelchair

Our feet creaked on wooden planks
in the dark, her makeshift ramp.
Her six-year-old son, Brandon,
opened the trailer door. A kettle steamed
on the stove from which Pam turned,
wheelchair-bound, to greet us.
After the accident her husband left her.
In the family portrait
that hung framed in a thin black frame
on the living room wall, his dark brown
wavy hair came down over his ears.
Dark eyes, dark clipped mustache.
Pam offered us coffee.
Brandon had gone to bed. I remember his
calling Pam through his bedroom wall.
Andy, tall, slightly stooped, prematurely
gray and balding, stood
and bumped his head on a ceiling lamp.
Pam's motorized chair hummed softly.
She reached for her Merit lights
on an end table.
Before Andy and I left the three of us
held hands and prayed
for Pam's well-being in Jesus' name.

Schaeffer Lights a Candle

In St Bartholomew's Church a stained-glass window
memorializes Carmine Zisa, a farmer who hanged himself
after a portion of his land was sold to developers
who built split level houses on that land.
But all the land wasn't sold, part was still left for farming.
Schaeffer wonders why Carmine wasn't content
to farm the remaining land. He wonders
if the farmer hanged himself because of the land
that he lost or for some other reason.
The candle Schaeffer lights is in the front of the church,
the stained glass is in the back.

What Is Lost Is Not Lost

I like looking at bicycles in old films
such as this one of Dawson, a mining town,
now a ghost town. I like at the opening
the long line of coke ovens, the miners, two
men, walking home from the mine. I like
the bicycles, the dogs, the women's dresses,
their hairstyles, looking into their faces
wondering what happened
after Dawson, where they went, what they
did or did not do, what they did or did not say.
The lady narrator, her
last name Loy, said she and her
husband went to graduate school the following year.
They had two young sons, Merrill, the elder,
and Bill, who lives now in Eugene,
Oregon, and introduces his mother
in the film, which was shot by Mr.
Loy in 1938. There are numerous shots
of the boys, several of Bill in his playpen
and then one where he seems
happy, having just
learned to walk. There are shots
of the mines, the houses that sprang from
mountainsides, the church, the school.
Now, nothing left in Dawson
but the cemetery. I like the moments of Bill
walking on his own,
but I have no idea what he does in Eugene.
He must almost be seventy.
His mother, a young wife
in the film, sticks her tongue out in
one shot. She was born in 1917.

Sign of the Jaguar

Deanna Shields
was a person of wealth and fame,
but died young from self-starvation.
A brunette beauty
whose talent in dance and singing
extended to acting,
she rode horses, excelled at tennis
and ballet. One New Year's Day,
a hunting accident changed everything;
the blast from her husband's gun
severed her spinal cord.
In her last film, *Sign of the Jaguar,*
she plays a wheelchair-bound wife,
the only difference was that in real life
by then Deanna was single.
In the film she is Kate Jameson.
At a mahogany desk her diary entry:
"make mine the mouth you kiss,
kiss of death," shows some
of what lies behind her genteel exterior:
seemingly kind but subtly cruel
to ones who warrant no cruelty
in this big Gothic house
which sits back from the sea.
The end is Kate emerging out of the fog.
At night in her wheelchair
she rolls toward a cliff.
Her whole being is in her eyes
that say:
I'll plunge through loneliness.
Where surf thrashes jagged rocks
a corpse bobs.
It won't be me, I'll be nowhere.

Nephritis

She was told his kidneys were not working
the way an eight-year-old's should.
She was crying. Light from the back yard
shone through the two dining room windows
and the one above the kitchen sink.
He would come home from the hospital
in two days. He would be bedridden
and need a tutor for the coming school year.
Her reading glasses lay on the table
in the shadow of the artificial flower
centerpiece. Worry filtered into wrinkles
in the corners of her brown eyes. Her left
hand, on her forehead, bore her wedding ring.
She wore no lipstick. Her arms and thin
shoulders bare, the shoulders curved
inward looking for an ocean, as if
it offered some escape from what
was to come when, hours later, the sky
darkened, and the supper dishes were drying
in a rack as she stood staring into the dark
out the kitchen window.

Pawn Shop

Between Flowers and Promise,
Mississippi, there's a pawn shop
and in it a gold bracelet
engraved to Jill from Clem.

When Jill died Clem crushed
a Marlboro into a metal tray.
It made a brushing sound.
The hand clasping his shoulder
made no sound. He stared
down a long white corridor.
She's with God now, said
the preacher. She's in heaven.

Hair

Ed Craig, the big mystery was we never saw the nuns' hair.
In classrooms, the convent, the big dark church
their hair stayed hidden.
You were bright, that showed in your grades.
Did you ever wonder what Sister James with her alabaster skin
and aquiline nose looked like with her habit off?
Her Sister of Charity habit's rim like white accordion pleats
squared her long face,
white pleats at the start of her long black habit.
Take the vow: don't show your hair,
the deal they made as Christ's brides. I never saw Sister's hair,
nor the hair of Sister Carmela or Sister Gerard or Sister Regina.
Sister Vincent, I heard, lives with a woman in New Hampshire.
How many left the convent, the order?
When habits' white pleats framed their faces the mass
was in Latin. When Latin left the mass the pleats were gone.
A round crescent circled faces different from ones
we answered to and obeyed.
Sister Vincent took off her habit in the convent.
I wanted her hair in my mouth.

The Fugitive

Driving home from softball
he hits a girl on a ten speed and keeps going.
Five hundred miles and one night later
his sister takes him in.

As she fixes him a gin and tonic
her husband lays sheets on a bed
that hasn't been slept in
since their daughter started school.

It was his fault, wasn't his fault.
The door said *Dazzling Disco.* In the dark
he hears his sister and her husband
downstairs, making love.

The Graveyard Shift

This is my son, Mr. Flores:
Eduardo, a good boy,
in second grade this year.

He was just one
when, the first day of class,
you called my name,

Estella Gutiérrez.
I raised my hand.
Then, absent from all classes,

absent forever.
My corpse found three days later,
shot, beaten, stabbed.

I didn't see my murderer, Mr. Flores.
As he broke my nose
blood trickled down my chin.

You stopped shopping at the Quick Stop,
as did others, outraged
that I was alone

on the graveyard shift.
I can't undo what's been done,
but if I could I'd tell Eduardo,

"Mind your sisters, stay in school."
Mr. Flores, my professor
for a day,

your *Essentials of Sociology*
lay open on the counter that night
I never heard the door open.

9/11

In Cather's story "Paul's Case,"
after the coach rides, the baths,
the tortoise shell brushes, mirrors,
satin sheets, chandeliers,
plush carpets, and ornate tables,
after the champagne and caviar feast,
Paul takes his baggage of flesh
draped in soft clothes
onto a final coach
into final woods, and down to the tracks,
and hurls himself into the path
of a locomotive,
choosing this form of death over poison,
pistol, or rope. It seems
he wants nothing to remain of Paul,
wants Paul himself obliterated,
wiped clean from earth's map,
no corpse, no likeness for mourners
to view and close the lid on,
and lower into an earthen hole.
Now, a hundred years after Cather's Paul,
a father named Paul bids his family
goodbye,
not knowing it's his final goodbye.
A farewell in the dark: he leans
to kiss his wife's cheek,
and then to the room of his sleeping son,
also Paul (an only child of an only child),
and leans and kisses his son's brow
and, with light approaching from the east,
walks out his gate and leaves
his familiar street, not knowing
the finalities of these minutes

remaining, unknown to him, this Paul
of September 2001, and to others
"on floor" when the plane crashes
through, and the sky falls
and turns into a celestial inferno.
Nothing left of September Paul
and those on his floor, nothing left
of the floor, or the shoes
he was wearing, or his teeth,
his wallet, nothing left there.
How could he have so much, one moment,
and then not even his teeth, his hair,
his family. How different his case
from that of Cather's brooding protagonist.

Schaeffer's Notion of Beauty

Bombs turn a building to rubble,
rescuers find
an arm, a leg.

In a mall a maniac fires a rifle,
leaving in his wake
dead children.

Hate manifestos
all over the Internet,
in the world there is danger:

a racist shoots Satyajit Chandra
at a bus stop
and nothing is done.

Still, even now, beauty
is with us.

Lucky Harmon

Lucky Harmon, he's out of it.
No worries about tuition, no frost
on a windshield, no bar mitzvah, no day
at the beach. No longer struts, dances,
sleeps, or opens the book *Around
the Corner.* These are words, said
the teacher, this is a page of words.
His book closed, ours are open. One day
a seashell to my ear, I heard the sea.
I imagine he did, too, but can't ask him.
The silence of the dead is ours, only.
He can't cry in a waiting room,
or at a daughter's side as the doctor
tells her "Because of gangrene we
have to amputate your leg." Can't ride
a board in gulf waters with a dog, gamble,
drink, chase skirts. No longer behind
a bar or anywhere, he's out of it. Others
are upset and will be with you and me.
Free to give and take, upset and make
others smile. As if he's in prison (for life)
and we're outside prison walls, free
to drop everything and go one sunny noon
into a dark Lowes cinema, the one
on Fordham Road he once reclined in,
one of the audience. He loved an audience!
No longer will I hear him sing, see him
dance in amateur light in his bedroom
with the bed unmade. Lucky Harmon.
Never to have been born is best.
How is it good never to have been born?
What about those who are born, suffer only,
and die? All they know is suffering, a bad
deal, tragic fate. Auden wrote
" . . . could not hope for help and no help
came." Life's mystery is at my fingertips,
What I was looking for was here.
We opened *Around the Corner.* The teacher
said, "Let's read the first sentence."

How Rich People Live

He was quite rich, but the big thing
he was rich in was how
he treated people, rich in humanity.

His spacious apartment
was bright with white sofas, chairs,
lamps and a white carpet, bright
and nuanced with shadows

that sunny Sunday afternoon.
I thought, This is how rich people live,
this is what it's like.

Also I thought
Whatever you do, don't mention the fight.
Yet, around one corner, on a wall
hung his championship belt from that fight

that resulted in another boxer's death.
Don't mention the fight. One moment
he got up from a chair. As he
walked by, I got up and said, Junior,

the name he went by, please
oblige me. For twenty seconds
I sparred with the great Emile Griffith.
He smiled, "Don't go into boxing."

That was my moment of fame,
feigning punches with this man whose
life was boxing, a man I knew
well enough to be

in his aesthetically pleasing digs
in a high rise
not far from the Lincoln Tunnel,
on the Jersey side of the Hudson.

In his early teens
he didn't want to box, but his handlers
knew how good he was.
Someone said he liked to be liked.

He liked to treat people well, for others
to treat him well, he liked giving
to his friends. He was, outside the ring,
easy going, gentle, and he liked

to laugh, and dance, and party.
He was gay. After the tragedy people
said he was fueled by anger because
Paret taunted him about being gay.

Paret's death was an accident.
It had nothing to do with revenge.
Griffith was only doing what
he'd trained to do.

Don't bring up the fight.
He never talked about it till they filmed
Ring of Fire. And he wept.
All those years it was eating him up

he'd taken a human life,
this kind and immensely talented man
who eventually lost the spacious digs,
the car and the friends.

Changing the Names

Johnny Frazier is in the same cemetery
as my parents.
With brick buildings, and sprawling lawn
it looked like a college campus.

Winter trees, the lawn snow
and headstones.
With each word out of my mouth
my breath coiled skyward.

I didn't try to find Johnny,
the best R&B singer ever,
on records
that showed his range. How easily

he modulates his voice, melodic,
distinct on ballads
such as "Harbor Lights" and jump tunes
like "Bim Bam."

He's there. So is James Owens,
right by my parents,
like them in a brick wall. A superstar
in the late eighties, early nineties.

Younger than I,
diabetes and its complications.
At my mom's burial,
a freezing January day, my sister said,

"James Owens"
and pointed to his name on a plaque.
Some voice.
I'm not saying Johnny's was better.

My parents heard neither singer,
well, maybe Johnny
when "Lover Please" played
every day, back in the day.

Enchantress

She casts a spell on a man.
She knows how. The secret
is in her dark flashing eyes,
and it is a secret.
She's not telling anyone.
It's better kept secret
from all, except herself.
She knows how.

Some things about herself
she doesn't know. But this one
she knows, for she must
because she does it very well.
What's her secret?
How does she cast her spell?
She's not telling.
Better not to whisper

even one word about it.
It happens slowly,
at times quickly, in silence.
It's good. The spell itself
is good. The man, as if
hypnotized, under her spell,
does what she wants,
which is fine, pleasing
both to him and her.

Enchantress, I imagine
sitting under a tarp
in the woods, out of the rain,
the rain all around me,
falling all around me.
That summer rain
is the nearness of you.

Acknowledgements

Poems in this collection either have appeared or will soon appear in the following publications:

Hospital: *Gulfstreaming*
Trotlines: *Common Ground Review*
GI, Water Elegies (originally Invisible Friends): *MSS*
Box: *Slant: A Journal of Poetry*
Blind Man Diving at Balmorhea, A Child Being Born, Boston Red Sox, Bobby Greenlease: *Neologism Poetry Journal*
To My Shrink, The Tylenol Murders: *The Mark Literary Review*
Among Women Only, Wishbone: *Mad Swirl*
The Translator: *Metafore Magazine*
Death, Sleep and the Traveler: *Detour Ahead* and *Home Planet News*
Horses Booze and Alimony, Changing the Names: *Home Planet News*
9/11: *Home Planet News, The Beautiful Space, The City Key,* and *Academy of the Heart and Mind*
Big: *Isthmus*
Purple Vest, What Is Lost Is Not Lost: *Zingara Poetry Review*
Pit Bull, Knives Lie on a Table, Slow Summer Night: *Black Petals*
My Shadow on a Rainy Day, Leon: *433*
Wishing Well: *The Nebraska Review*
Schaeffer and the Stones, Schaeffer Lights a Candle: *The Magnolia Review*
Shreveport Phone Booth, Mike Tyson Inside, Tweakers: *Misery Tourism*
Ham Radio, Sign of the Jaguar: *Avatar Review*
Flames: *Agony Opera* and *Avatar Review*
Gospel: *The BeZine* and *Avatar Review*
Schaeffer's Notion of Beauty: *The BeZine, Masque & Spectacle,* and *Artvilla*

The Gradebook, Stone Floor, River: *Academy of the Heart and Mind*
First Haircut: *Beliveau Review* and *Academy of the Heart and Mind*
His Vietnam Tour: *Collateral*
Damp Wallet: *Yolk Literary Journal* and *Fine Lines*
Knock on Wood: *Offcourse Literary Journal*
The Broom: *Offcourse Literary Journal* and *The Moth Magazine*
Chow: *Pinyon Review*
White Wine, Pull Over, Nephritis: *Adelaide Literary Magazine*
Schaeffer Is Next: *Bluepepper, Agony Opera* and *Artvilla*
Justine: *Ariel Chart*
Guard Dog: *Burrow e journal*
Jeremiah (originally Brown Shoes): *Colere*
Prayer: *Bez & Co*
Pawn Shop: *Frugal Chariot*
Hair, Enchantress: *BOMBFIRE*
The Fugitive: *Wind Magazine*
The Graveyard Shift: *The Poetry Village*
Lucky Harmon: *The Alchemy Spoon*
How Rich People Live: *Nude Bruce Review* and *45 Magazine*

About the Author

Peter Mladinic lives in Hobbs, New Mexico. He was born and raised in New Jersey and has lived in the Midwest and in the South. He enlisted in the United States Navy and served for four years. He received an MFA in Creative Writing from the University of Arkansas in 1985, and taught English for thirty years at New Mexico Junior College in Hobbs. He has edited two books: *Love, Death, and the Plains* and *Ethnic Lea: Southeast New Mexico Stories,* which are available from the Lea County Museum Press, as are his three volumes of poetry: *Lost in Lea, Dressed for Winter,* and his most recent book, co-authored with Charles Behlen, *Falling Awake in Lovington.* He is a past board member of the Lea County Museum and a former president of the Lea County Humane Society. An animal activist, he supports numerous animal rescue groups. Two of his main concerns are to bring an end to the euthanizing of animals in shelters and to help get animals in shelters adopted into caring homes. In his spare time, he enjoys yoga, listening to music, reading, and spending time with his six dogs. Recently, his poems have been published in numerous online journals in the US, Canada, England, Ireland, and Australia.

www.ingramcontent.com/pod-product-compliance
Lightning Source LLC
Chambersburg PA
CBHW072207100526
44589CB00015B/2406